SHE CAN'T BUY YOU GIFTS

YOU GIFTS

NADIA SOUINI

Dedication

This book is dedicated to every stay-at-home mom.
You are seen and appreciated.

About the Author

It was a regular day in the suburbs of Dubai. I was rocking my baby and scrolling through my phone when I came across a story online that shook me to my core. It was about a child who preferred his working stepmom over his stay-at-home mother because she could buy him gifts and take him on trips, while his mother could not.

To say my world fell apart would not be an exaggeration. Could all the sacrifices I am making go unnoticed just because they can't be wrapped in gift paper? How many women feel the same way?

It became crucial to me that children understand and appreciate everything their mothers do, without comparing them to others just because they can't buy gifts. A mother herself is the gift—God's gift.

That realization inspired me to write this book.

For who she was. She can no longer be.

She gave up her career and now works many jobs for free.

Because she wants to make sure you are safe and happy.

For you, there isn't a place she would not go.

From when you were a baby until you become a man.

For a mother's love is second to none.

Mommy loves you.

ACTIVITY STARTS HERE...

Find the Son?

Find the Mom?

Find Words With Friends?

Cat
Chicken
Donkey
Dog
Cow
Horse
Hen

Solve Them

2 + 4 =

4 + 2 =

6 - 4 =

6 - 2 =

1 2 3 4 5 6 7 8 9 10

Find Your Way

START

FINISH

Puzzle For Kids

Game For Kids

Spelling Words Scramble

N O S   M M O